Koprince Law LLC GovCon Handbooks

Volume 3:

Debriefings and Bid Protests

A Guide to Protest Rules and Regulations– In Plain English

Matthew T. Schoonover & Matthew P. Moriarty

Nothing contained in this book is to be considered as the rendering of legal advice for specific cases, and readers are responsible for obtaining such advice from their own legal counsel. This book is intended for educational and information purposes only. Although the authors strive to present accurate information, the information provided in this book is not guaranteed to be accurate, complete, or up-to-date. Buying or reading this book does not establish an attorney-client relationship with the authors and/or Koprince Law LLC.

© 2019 Matthew T. Schoonover & Matthew P. Moriarty
All rights reserved
Published March 2019

The authors gratefully acknowledge the hard work of Abigail Case in proofreading, formatting, and publishing this GovCon Handbook.

Contents

INTRODUCTION 1
- ABOUT THIS SERIES 3
- DISCLAIMERS! 4
- LET'S GET STARTED 6

PART I – DEBRIEFINGS 7
- WHAT IS A DEBRIEFING? 8
- WHEN ARE DEBRIEFINGS REQUIRED? 13
- TIMELINESS OF A BID PROTEST 15
- DEBRIEFINGS UNDER DEPARTMENT OF DEFENSE ACQUISITIONS 19

PART II – BID PROTESTS 26
- WHAT IS A BID PROTEST? 27
- WHO CONSIDERS A BID PROTEST? 30
  - Agency-Level Protests 30
- PRE-AWARD BID PROTESTS 36
  - Government Accountability Office 37
  - Court of Federal Claims 44
- THE TAKEAWAY 47
- POST-AWARD BID PROTESTS 49
  - Government Accountability Office 51
  - Court of Federal Claims 64
- INTERVENTION: DEFENDING YOUR AWARD 68
- CONCLUSION 73
- ACRONYMS LIST 74
- BIOS 78

INTRODUCTION

Uncle Sam is the world's single largest purchaser of goods and services. Every year, the federal government spends about *half a trillion dollars* of the items it needs to maintain its daily operations—everything from aircraft carriers and fighter jets, to ballpoint pens and toilet paper, to IT services and aerial firefighting services. It buys these items through thousands upon thousands of contracts or orders.

Each of these awards is, in and of itself, a significant effort. Not only for the government, but also for offerors. And if your business has submitted a proposal or quote on a procurement, you know this to be true: even the simplest bids can take hours upon hours to prepare.

It's only natural, then, that a company that loses out on an award would be upset and, if they think the award was improper, file a bid protest. And bid protests play an important part of the acquisition system. Sure, there exists the generalized belief that too many protests might delay acquisitions or make them more expensive. In fact, just a few years ago, Congress directed that the

Department of Defense commission a study on the effect of bid protests on acquisitions as a whole.[1] The results of that study (which we'll touch on a little later) actually shows this generalized belief to be more myth than reality: overall, just a fraction of contract awards are protested annually, with relatively high degrees of success.

The reality is that bid protests help ensure acquisitions are conducted fairly and reasonably. Even still, many contractors (and, presumably, many contracting officers) shudder when they hear those two words.

That's where this *GovCon Handbook* comes in. Together, we'll walk through bid protests—we'll discuss what they are, where they can (or even should) be filed, the protest process, potential arguments (and arguments to avoid), and possible outcomes. We'll also discuss some of the statistics to give a better

---

[1] 2017 National Defense Authorization Act, Pub. L. 114-328, § 885, 103 Stat. 2000, 2319 (2016). A quick note: each year, Congress passes the National Defense Authorization Act (or *NDAA* for short), which basically sets out the funding and policy priorities for the military. Each NDAA is chock full of provisions relating to federal contracting. And though these provisions are only immediately applicable to DoD, they're nonetheless relevant to federal contracting as a whole. So, we'll talk in this *Handbook* about NDAAs from various years.

sense of how many protests are filed annually and the overall potential for success.

Before diving into the deep end, we'll first briefly touch on debriefings. Why? Well, a debriefing is often the prelude to a bid protest, as it's through a debriefing (or brief explanation of award, as the case may be) that an offeror learns the basis for the evaluation and award decision. If unsatisfied with that explanation—either in form or in substance—an offeror might be more inclined to file a protest. And beyond that, debriefings can play a crucial role in determining the timeliness of a protest.

It's our hope that this information will help better explain the protest process so that your company can be prepared if it finds itself in that situation.

About this Series

This *GovCon Handbook* is the third volume in a series that we and our colleagues are publishing.[2] Future editions, like this one, will cover government contracts topics in-depth.

---

[2] The first two editions, *Government Contracts Joint Ventures* and *SBA Small Business Size and Affiliation Rules*, are available on Amazon.

As each *GovCon Handbook* is published, we'll alert you on our blog, *SmallGovCon* (smallgovcon.com). We've been writing *SmallGovCon* since 2012, and we're at 1,250 posts and counting. *SmallGovCon* is written much like this book: a lot of information, a minimum of legalese, and the occasional bad joke. We hope that you'll check it for the latest government contracting news.

Disclaimers!

Before we go any further, let's pause for three important disclaimers.

First, as the text at the front boldly states, this *GovCon Handbook* is intended for your educational use only. Though this book will discuss the generalities of filing a bid protest, and will often cite past bid protest decisions as guides, you should know that no two bid protests are alike. The facts of each solicitation and evaluation vary, and differences in circumstances can impact the analysis of any potential bid protest. Just because one protest challenging, say, a flawed price realism evaluation is sustained doesn't mean that every other price realism challenge will also be sustained. And we're not writing this *Handbook* to encourage every disappointed offeror to challenge every lost award. Instead, we simply want to provide information about the complex world of bid protests, to help demystify them to our readers.

Second, and along the lines of the first point, buying this book, or simply reading it, does not create an attorney-client relationship between you (the reader) and us (Koprince Law LLC). The content in this *Handbook* is not intended to be legal advice. If you have specific questions about a bid protest—either bringing a protest or defending your award against one—we recommend that you seek competent counsel. It doesn't have to be us (though, don't get us wrong, we'd take your call); but please, don't rely on this book for legal advice.

Third, like most things in life, the government contracting rules sometimes change, and bid protest decisions are overruled or distinguished. This *GovCon Handbook* reflects the rules as they were in early 2019. Depending on when you're reading this *Handbook*, some of what's discussed in this book might be out of date. Keep an eye on our blog (*SmallGovCon*) for the latest information about bid protests. And, again, if you're involved in a protest, consider getting legal help.

Let's Get Started

With the disclaimers out of the way, it's time to get started. First, let's quickly discuss debriefings. Then we'll get into the meat of this *Handbook* and talk about bid protests.

Part I – DEBRIEFINGS

You've submitted a bid on a federal contract, pouring a lot of time (and money) to developing the strongest bid possible. But at the end of the day, you have no idea whether the government will love or hate it. Sure, you'll get some sense when the award is announced—if the agency awards you the contract, it probably liked your proposed effort; if someone else wins, maybe it didn't—but win or lose, how are you supposed to know how to make it better next time?

A simple thumbs up or thumbs down isn't sufficient or fair—after all, you've spent hours, maybe days preparing a proposal and deserve an explanation why the agency awarded, or didn't award, you the contract.

Here's the good news: The government agrees. That's where a debriefing comes in.

At its most basic, a debriefing is an agency's explanation of how it viewed an offeror's proposal and why it selected a particular company to perform a contract. But not only that, a debriefing also plays a critical role in the bid protest process, helping a potential protester learn whether or not a protest would have any legs and, also, when it should be filed.

In this part, we'll briefly discuss debriefings—what they are, when they're required (and when they're not), and their role in the protest process. At the conclusion of this part, we'll also discuss tips to make the most of your debriefing.

WHAT IS A DEBRIEFING?

At the outset, let's address the fundamental question: *what is a debriefing*? As mentioned above, a debriefing is simply a summary of the agency's evaluation decisions. Conducted properly, debriefings provide offerors with basic information about the evaluation and award, what the agency liked, did not like, and what led to the ultimate award decision. They also provide significant insight into any potential mistakes the agency made. A significant number of bid protests are based on information learned in a debriefing.

Debriefings come in two types: pre-award and post-award. A pre-award debriefing, as its name suggests, is provided to offerors that were eliminated from competition as part of the establishment of a competitive range. In other words, say there are 10 offerors that submit a bid under a solicitation to provide laundry and dry-cleaning services at Fort Jackson, South Carolina. If the government believes that evaluating all 10 proposals would be too burdensome or unwieldy, it might decide to establish a competitive range cutoff. Assume that 4 of the proposals were clearly superior—in the government's preliminary evaluation—to the remaining 6. Those 4 proposals would establish the competitive range (and proceed to the next phase of the evaluation, perhaps with the opportunity to participate in discussions), while the remaining 6 that were not rated as highly would be eliminated from further competition (and thus not evaluated any further). These 6 offerors, then, might get a pre-award debriefing.

What information would be included in this pre-award debriefing? The Federal Acquisition Regulation (or *FAR*, in government-contracting lingo) provides the answer: a pre-award debriefing must include—

    1. The agency's evaluation of significant elements in the offeror's proposal;

2. A summary of the rationale for eliminating the offeror from the competition; and

3. Reasonable responses to relevant questions about whether source selection procedures contained in the solicitation, applicable regulations, or other applicable authorities were followed in the process of eliminating the offeror from the competition.

FAR 15.505(e)(1).

Importantly, the FAR also sets out various pieces of information that a pre-award debriefing <u>cannot</u> include. These prohibitions include the number or name of the other offerors, the evaluation or ranking of those offerors, any content from the other offerors' proposals, or any other proprietary or trade secret information. <u>Id.</u> at 15.505(f).

So with that, offerors excluded from the competitive range should receive at least a basic understanding of the perceived issues with their proposals. True, these offerors won't receive a comparison of their proposal to that of the winner, but this information should at least give a sense of why the proposal was ultimately excluded.

What about the remaining 4 offerors that did advance past the competitive range cutoff? An evaluation following a competitive range cutoff is, naturally, going to be more substantive than the evaluation conducted as part of the competitive range cutoff, so these offerors will receive more information as part of their debriefings. Again, the FAR provides the information that must be included:

1. The Government's evaluation of significant weaknesses or deficiencies in the offeror's proposal, if applicable;

2. The overall evaluated cost or price (including unit prices) and technical rating, if applicable, of the successful offeror and the debriefed offeror, and past performance information on the debriefed offeror;

3. The overall ranking of offerors, when any ranking was developed by the agency during the source selection;

4. A summary of the rationale for award;

5. For acquisitions of commercial items, the make and model of the item to be delivered by the successful offeror; and

6. Reasonable responses to relevant questions about whether source selection procedures in the solicitation, applicable regulations, and other applicable authorities were followed.

Id. at 15.506(d).

But as with pre-award debriefings, an agency is prohibited from providing certain information as part of a post-award debriefing. Specifically, an agency cannot disclose a point-by-point comparison of proposals. And, of course, an agency cannot disclose any confidential or proprietary information. Id. at 15.506(e).

So the answer to the question of *what's a debriefing?* is relatively straightforward: it's the agency's explanation of the award decision. Depending on the type of debriefing—pre-award or post-award—the level of detail in the explanation might differ. But if conducted properly, the debriefed offeror should leave the debriefing with a better understanding of the award decision.

> **KEEP IN MIND**
>
> Our discussion in this handbook presumes that disappointed offerors will ask for a debriefing. But keep in mind that awardees are also entitled to debriefings, too.
>
> Should you ask for a debriefing if you win the contract? Absolutely! Sure, earning the award generally tells you that the agency liked your proposal. But a debriefing will explain what specifically the agency liked and why it decided to give you the award. Armed with this information, you might be able to improve your odds under future procurements.

WHEN ARE DEBRIEFINGS REQUIRED?

Knowing what a debriefing is, however, is only partially helpful. Contractors should also know when an agency is required to give a debriefing. That answer isn't as simple as it might seem. And, as we'll see, whether an agency is required to give a debriefing is vitally important to the bid protest process.

Although the benefits of receiving a debriefing are universal, the FAR only mandates that a debriefing be offered under two types of procurements: in negotiated procurements (conducted under FAR Part 15) and whenever the agency awards a task order valued at $5.5 million or more (per FAR 16.505(b)(6)).

For every other type of procurement—GSA schedule buys (under FAR Part 8), commercial item acquisitions (FAR Part 12), simplified acquisitions (FAR Part 13), and sealed bidding (FAR Part 14)—debriefings are not required; instead, an agency only needs to provide offerors in these acquisitions a "brief explanation of award."

Substantively, a brief explanation might not be much different than a debriefing. In some instances, the agency provides information that explains why it made its award decision. Other times, however, the agency provides very little information to the unsuccessful offeror—maybe little more than a terse statement to the effect of "We awarded the contract to the proposal we liked best."

Whether a debriefing is required or not is vitally important information, for two reasons. First, the debriefing provides helpful information about the award determination. While they may lead to the contractor discovering the basis of a protest ground, the ostensible purpose of offering a debriefing is that the information will serve to help the debriefed offeror improve for future procurements. Indeed, debriefings may actually cut down on bid protests because they prevent a disappointed offeror from filing a bid protest simply to find out why they did not win. Post-debrief, the offeror has a better understanding of the strengths and weaknesses of its approach. The offeror is thereafter in a better position to incorporate those strengths under future solicitations while, at the same time, mitigating identified risks. By being willing to share this information, the government puts the offeror in a better position to win the next solicitation.

Second, when required, a debriefing dramatically affects the timeliness of a bid protest, as we'll explore below.

TIMELINESS OF A BID PROTEST

Debriefings play a crucial role in determining when a bid protest is due.

16 | Debriefings and Bid Protests

The deadline to file a protest challenging an evaluation or award[3] is relatively straightforward: for procurements where a debriefing is both **required** and **timely requested**, a bid protest is due **10 calendar days after the debriefing**. For all other procurements (or where a debriefing is not timely requested), a bid protest is due within 10 days from the date the offeror learns of the grounds of protest. A protest will be dismissed if it's filed outside of this deadline (say, on the 11th day after the protester received its timely-requested and required debriefing).

When is a debriefing timely requested? For pre-award debriefings, an offeror must request its debriefing within 3 *calendar days* from the date it receives notice of its exclusion from the competitive range. FAR 15.505(a)(1).[4] For post-award debriefings, an offeror must request the debriefing within 3

---

[3] This is the rule for GAO protests challenging an agency's evaluation or award decisions. Protests challenging the terms of a solicitation must be filed before the deadline to submit proposals. Note, also, that the timeliness rules for post-award bid protests at the Court of Federal Claims vary substantially from GAO's rules.

[4] An offeror can elect to receive its pre-award debriefing after the agency makes its award determination. This could be a trap! A protest challenging the exclusion of an offeror from the competitive range might be considered untimely if that offeror waits to protest until it receives a post-award debriefing. Generally, a pre-award debriefing should take place as soon as possible, without waiting for the final award determination.

calendar days from the date it receives notice of the award. FAR 15.506(a)(1).

> **EXAMPLE**
>
> Elliott, the contracting officer under a FAR Part 15 procurement seeking IT support services, sends Stellar Technology, Inc. notification of the award on Friday at 3:38 p.m. Molly, Stellar's president, emails Elliott on Monday at noon to request Stellar's debriefing.
>
> **Result:** Stellar's debriefing request is timely. The first calendar day was Saturday; the second, Sunday; and third, Monday. If Stellar chooses to file a protest, the deadline will be 10 days from the date it receives the debriefing.

18 | Debriefings and Bid Protests

> **EXAMPLE**
>
> Caleb, the contracting officer under a FAR Part 15 procurement for dog food manufacturing, sends Puppy Feast notification of the award on Friday at 3:38 p.m. Leah, Puppy Feast's point of contact, is out of the office and doesn't return until Tuesday. She immediately responds and requests a debriefing.
>
> **Result:** Puppy Feast's debriefing request is not timely. Although Caleb can still provide a debriefing, Puppy Feast's deadline to file a protest will be 10 days from the date it learned of the evaluation flaw—not 10 days from the date it receives the debriefing.

Where possible, we think it's a best practice to *immediately* request a debriefing under *every* procurement. Beyond being in writing, a debriefing request doesn't have to be in any special form. All that's required is some variation of four magic words: "We request a debriefing."[5]

---

[5] In our experience, most contracting officers provide evaluation notices by email. In that case, requesting a debriefing can be as simple as hitting "Reply All" and asking for one. If the contracting officer provides notice by mail, an offeror should email a written request to the contracting officer as soon as that notice is received.

DEBRIEFINGS UNDER DEPARTMENT OF DEFENSE ACQUISITIONS

Up to this point, our discussion about debriefings has been relatively straightforward. Debriefings are required only under a few types of procurements [negotiated acquisitions and orders valued more than $5.5 million] and, if timely requested [within 3 calendar days from the date of the evaluation notification], impact the deadline to file a protest [making the protest due within 10 days from the date of receiving the debriefing]. But Congress has recently complicated things a bit.

As part of the 2018 National Defense Authorization Act, Congress mandated "enhanced debriefings" under most Department of Defense acquisitions.[6] In doing so, Congress significantly expanded the situations in which the agency must provide "a written or oral debriefing for *all* contract awards and task or delivery orders valued at $10,000,000 or higher."

---

[6] Again, this portion of the 2018 NDAA only applies to the Department of Defense, so the "enhanced debriefings" only apply to defense agencies, not civilian ones.

2018 NDAA, Pub. L. No. 115-91, § 818(a)(2), 131 Stat. 1283, 1463 (2017).[7]

In these cases, moreover, the agency must provide a copy of its source selection decision document (redacted to remove any other offeror's confidential information) as part of the debriefing. What's more, the agency <u>must</u> allow the offeror to submit questions <u>after</u> it receives its debriefing, and then answer those questions within five days. For procurements covered by this new "enhanced debriefing" requirement, the offeror's protest clock doesn't start running until it receives the agency's answers to these questions.

///

---

[7] This provision has been codified at 10 U.S.C. § 2305. Neither the FAR nor DFARS have been formally updated to implement the provision, but the Department of Defense has issued a class waiver to implement its terms in the interim.

> **EXAMPLE**
>
> Force Protection Services submitted a sealed bid (under FAR Part 14) to construct base security fortifications at Fort Benning. On May 1, Force Protection learned that a different small business was awarded the contract, for $10,500,000, and immediately requested its debriefing.
>
> On May 5, the Army provided Force Protection with its written debriefing. On May 7, Force Protection asked the Army questions about the evaluation (following its review of the debriefing), and received those answers on May 10.
>
> **Result:** Under the 2018 NDAA, Force Protection's bid protest clock begins running on May 10. To be timely, its protest would have to be filed by May 20.

As this example shows, the 2018 NDAA imposes a significant change to the debriefing requirements for Department of Defense procurements. Again, this is only for solicitations that are issued by the Department of Defense—it does not apply to any civilian procurements. So, if your procurement is issued by, say, the Department of Veterans Affairs or the Department of the Interior, you'll need to follow the same debriefing rules discussed earlier.

***

So that's it—the basics about debriefings. With this (brief) discussion, we hope you learned a bit more about the debriefing process. Beyond that, we hope you understand a bit more about their role in the bid protest process—not only might a debriefing help shed light on any potential grounds for a bid protest, but also the debriefing itself might impact the deadline to file a protest.

Before moving on to the broader bid protest discussion, we wanted to wrap up this topic by providing our suggestions for a successful debriefing. This isn't intended to be a comprehensive list, as your particular situation might lead to additional or alternative considerations. But with the following in mind, hopefully you'll have set yourself up for a successful debriefing.

1. *Immediately request your debriefing.* To be timely, a debriefing has to be requested within 3 calendar days from the date you receive notice of the evaluation determination. We suggest that, once the contracting officer notifies you of that

decision, you should immediately respond (in writing) with a clear request for a debriefing. And again, avoid the "pre-award exclusion/post-award debriefing" trap—if your proposal is eliminated from the competitive range, ask that your debriefing occur as soon as possible, without waiting for the actual award determination.

2. *Decide whether you'd like the debriefing to be written or oral.* A contracting officer might ask whether you'd like your debriefing to be written or oral. If so, the answer will largely depend on your personal preference. But if you choose an oral debriefing (or if the contracting officer chooses an oral debriefing for you), have a dedicated note-taker present.

3. *Re-familiarize yourself with the solicitation and your proposal.* An evaluation might take weeks or months to complete. By the time the award is made and a debriefing is conducted, you'll likely have forgotten some aspects of the procurement. So, we suggest that you refamiliarize yourself with the procurement before the debriefing—have your proposal team meet to discuss the solicitation, your effort, and to discuss why your company offered the solution it did.

4. *Consider any questions and submit them to the contracting officer.* After refamiliarizing yourself with the solicitation and your proposal, what questions about the evaluation might you have? Write them down and ask the contracting officer if you can submit them for her consideration.

5. *Maintain a professional demeanor.* No matter what happens in a debriefing, it's important to remain professional—even if you're intending to file a bid protest. This can sometimes be difficult, especially when the contracting officer doesn't meet your professionalism halfway. But even still, leaving the best impression with the agency can never hurt.

6. *Have an after-action plan to implement lessons learned.* This is, perhaps, the most important tip for debriefings. All-too-often, we see contractors view the debriefing as simply a prelude to a protest. While that's true in a sense, it misses the larger picture: a debriefing is designed to help an offeror better understand the evaluation of its proposal so that it might better position itself for the award on the next procurement.

To make the most of a debriefing, we recommend that a contractor develop an after-action plan to implement these lessons. Discuss the debriefing findings with your proposal team.

What strengths can you implement from this effort into similar efforts in the future? And how might you mitigate any risks or weaknesses found under this proposal so that you don't end up repeating them? Should you consider teaming with another entity to help plug any gaps in your capabilities or experience? These are important questions your team should consider—if it doesn't, you've wasted an opportunity to improve your shot at winning the next award.

✳✳✳

That's it for debriefings. Up next, we'll get to the heart of the matter and discuss the ins-and-outs of bid protests.

PART II – BID PROTESTS

Now that we've covered debriefings and their role to the bid protest process, let's talk about protests themselves.

When we first began writing this *Handbook*, we started with the assumption that readers would have at least a basic understanding of government contracts. After all, who would *choose* to read about government contracts *other than government contractors*? But upon further reflection, this assumption isn't fair: this book is designed, after all, to provide the basics about government contracts. We hope it's equally useful to experienced and hopeful government contractors alike. What's more, in our practice, we get calls from experienced government contractors who have (luckily enough for them) never been involved in a bid protest.

With this in mind, it's appropriate to start at first principles:

WHAT IS A BID PROTEST?

At its most basic, a bid protest is a challenge to an agency's procurement-related decision. Protests generally come in two types: pre-award and post-award. We'll break down each type in more detail below, but in general, a *pre-award protest* challenges a solicitation, while a *post-award* protest challenges an agency's evaluation.

EXAMPLE

BigPlanes owns an awesome feat of engineering—a Boeing 747 that has been converted to hold and deploy nearly 20,000 gallons of fire suppressant. It uses this airplane to assist with aerial firefighting efforts, so it was miffed when the U.S. Forest Service issued a solicitation seeking aerial firefighting services that restricted the volume of suppressant capacity to a meager 5000 gallons. Based on that restriction, BigPlanes would not be able to offer the use of its converted 747.

Result: BigPlanes likely has a valid basis to file a pre-award protest to challenge the agency's restrictive solicitation requirement. In fact, we know it would. This example cribs from a recent GAO decision sustaining a protest challenging a similar requirement. See Global SuperTanker Services, LLC, B-414987 et al., 2017 CPD ¶ 345 (Comp. Gen. Nov. 6, 2017).

///

EXAMPLE

Happy Trains recently learned that its proposal to repair a railcar on behalf of the Federal Railroad Administration was not awarded a contract. According to its debriefing, the government thought Happy Trains' price was so unrealistically low Happy Trains either could not do the work for that price or did not understand the extent of the job. The solicitation, however, was issued on a fixed-price basis and didn't warn offerors that their price could be too low.

Result: Happy Trains has a viable post-award protest ground, as the agency probably shouldn't have evaluated for price realism without letting offerors know it would. If it would like to challenge the evaluation, it should file a protest. See Crawford RealStreet Joint Venture, B-415193.2 et al., 2018 CPD ¶ 121 (Comp. Gen. Apr. 2, 2018) (sustaining protest where agency performed price realism analysis under a fixed-price solicitation, when offerors weren't told that prices would be evaluated for realism).

WHO CONSIDERS A BID PROTEST?

Beyond knowing what a bid protest is, it's also important to know how a bid protest is considered. Regardless of the type of protest, there are generally three forums[8] in which a protest can be filed: the agency itself, the Government Accountability Office (or GAO),[9] or the United States Court of Federal Claims (*COFC*).

AGENCY-LEVEL PROTESTS

Before we dig into the differences between a pre-award and post-award protest, we first want to explain agency-level protests. Uniquely, agency-level protests are resolved by the agency itself. That is, the protester sends its challenge to the contracting officer,

---

[8] I know what you're thinking: *Isn't the plural of "forum" actually "fora"?* Yes, it is. But *forums* is also acceptable. Trust me, I looked it up. See *Fora vs. forums*, Grammarist, available at https://grammarist.com/usage/fora-forums/ (last viewed Dec. 19, 2018).

[9] Protests relating to solicitations issued by the Federal Aviation Administration cannot be filed at GAO. Instead, those protests are considered by the FAA's Office of Dispute Resolution for Acquisition. We won't get into FAA protests in this *Handbook*, but we would be happy to discuss any questions you might have about them.

who then has a soft 35-day deadline to issue a decision on the protest ("soft," because the FAR only requires an agency to make its "best efforts" to resolve a protest within this time). Unlike a protest at GAO or the COFC, a protester (or its counsel) isn't entitled to any document production by the agency. Although we don't have any empirical data to support this point, it's our experience that agency-level protests aren't all that common. It makes sense, because an agency-level protest is decided by the body that just made the decision the protester is challenging. There's no truly impartial third-party decider, although the FAR does allow the protester to request a review at a level above the contracting officer.

Even still, an agency-level protest might be appropriate in a few instances. For example, consider a situation in which the agency issued a solicitation that has an obvious error—maybe the solicitation cover page says that the solicitation is set-aside for woman-owned small businesses, but the PWS says it's set-aside for SDVOSBs. If informal efforts to resolve the inconsistency go unanswered, a protester might consider an agency-level protest to quickly resolve the issue (and maybe save the agency any perceived embarrassment for having such an obvious goof pointed out publicly). Another consideration might be the protester's relationship with the agency itself: in some cases, a protester fears that a protest might spoil its goodwill with an agency. In that case, raising concerns of an improper evaluation through an agency-level protest might be appropriate.

Bear in mind that the choice of the protest forum isn't a one-time decision. That is, a protester might first choose to file an agency-level protest and, if that's not successful, then file its challenge at GAO. And if that GAO protest isn't successful, the protester might then protest at the Court of Federal Claims, meaning that a protester might get a few bites at the apple. But this "pecking order" doesn't work in reverse: once a protest is filed at COFC, a protester can't then go to GAO or the agency. Neither can a protester file an agency-level protest after unsuccessfully raising its challenge at GAO.

With that background, let's focus a bit on the mechanics of an agency-level protest. The following applies for both pre-award and post-award agency-level protests:

- o **When to file?** FAR 33.103(e) sets forth the deadlines for agency-level protests. A *pre-award* protest (or, again, a challenge to the solicitation's terms or the structure of the procurement) must be filed at the agency "before bid opening or the closing date for the receipt of proposals"—in other words, you must file a pre-award protest before your proposal is due. A *post-award* protest (challenging the evaluation or award) must be filed "no later than 10 days after the basis of protest is known or should have been known, whichever is earlier."

- <u>What to file?</u> An agency-level protest must be in writing and include at least the following information:
  - The protester's name, address, and fax number;[10]
  - The solicitation or contract number;
  - Information supporting the protester's status as an interested party with standing to protest and the timeliness of the protest;
  - <u>If seeking a review at a level above the contracting officer, a statement of that request;</u>
  - A detailed description of the factual and legal basis (or bases) for protest, an explanation of any

---

[10] Yes, the FAR requires a fax number . . . still. If you have a fax number, you should include it. If not, be sure to include any other contact information you might have—at a minimum, your phone number and email address.

prejudice suffered by the protester, and copies of relevant documents supporting these assertions; and

- An "ask," or an explanation of the relief sought.

FAR 33.103(d)(2).

- o Where to file? An agency-level protest must be sent to the contracting officer or to the agency official designated to receive protests (check the solicitation). FAR 33.103(d)(3).
- o Resolution. As mentioned, the agency has a "soft" 35-day deadline to resolve an agency-level protest. FAR 33.103(g). Its decision "shall be well-reasoned and explain the agency position." FAR 33.103(f).

That's the nuts and bolts about agency-level protests. Again, unlike GAO or COFC protests, there is not much available data about how often they're filed or how effective they might be. Candidly, we're skeptical of their utility—usually, agencies put a lot of thought into their procurements, so asking them to reconsider doesn't seem like the best use of time or money. Instead, GAO or COFC protests seem much more common. Although resolution might not come as fast, at least those forums provide an impartial third-party decider and allow an offeror (through its counsel) the ability to obtain procurement-related documents that might help "stress test" an agency's position.

If you do file an unsuccessful agency-level protest, although it preserves the right to file a GAO protest, the deadline is a short one: ordinarily, a subsequent GAO protest must be filed "within 10 days of actual or constructive knowledge" of an adverse decision by the agency. 4 C.F.R. § 21.2(a)(3).

***

In the remainder of this *Handbook*, we'll focus on GAO and COFC protests. We'll do so by looking at various requirements and considerations for each forum based on the type of protest being pursued. We'll then conclude as we did in the last Part, by offering tips for bid protests.

PRE-AWARD BID PROTESTS

It's 7:38 a.m. You've just sat at your desk at the dog food manufacturing company, with a fresh cup of coffee. After checking Twitter,[11] you log on to *FedBizOpps* to check for the latest solicitations in your industry.[12] Finding one, you eagerly start reviewing its requirements. *That's odd*, you think, *why does the government want this dog food to be made entirely out of dark chocolate?*

Either Uncle Sam is a cat person, or the agency made a mistake. But it seems like you have grounds for a viable pre-award protest.

A pre-award protest is, again, a challenge to the ground rules of a solicitation. This challenge could focus on the specifications offered by the agency (like a requirement to make dog food out of dark chocolate, in our example) or the structure of the competition itself (for example, the failure to set aside a

---

[11] You can follow *SmallGovCon* or your authors: @SmallGovCon; @mtschoonover; and @MoriartyGovCon.

[12] Believe it or not, the government buys dog food. Check out Solicitation 112639519Q0030, issued by the Department of Agriculture on November 15, 2018, under NAICS code 311111 (Dog and Cat Food Manufacturing).

solicitation for small businesses). The thrust: if there's something about the solicitation itself that might impact your ability to intelligently or fairly compete for the award, you should consider a pre-award protest.

After deciding to file a pre-award protest, the next task is to decide where to file it. We discussed considerations for agency-level protests above. Now, let's consider a bit more about protests at GAO and the Court of Federal Claims.

GOVERNMENT ACCOUNTABILITY OFFICE

In all candor, the mechanics of a GAO protest aren't all that different than an agency-level protest filing. The *path to resolution* is different, but the initial protest filing is relatively similar:

- When to file? GAO's bid protest regulations require that a protest alleging "improprieties in a solicitation which are apparent prior to bid opening or the time set for receipt of initial proposals" must be filed no later than "bid opening or the time set for receipt of initial proposals." 4 C.F.R. § 21.2(a)(1). In other words, if the solicitation is ambiguous, or if its terms are either unreasonable or unfair, you have to file your protest before the deadline to submit proposals. Given this deadline, it's important to know the exact time that proposals are due. For example, if a proposal is due at 12:00 p.m. (Eastern) on December 12, a protest that is filed at 12:01 p.m. or after will be considered untimely—and dismissed.[13]

- **What to file?** A GAO protest must be in writing and include the following information:
    - The protester's name, address, telephone and fax numbers, and email address;
    - Identification of the agency and the solicitation or contract number;
    - Information supporting the protester's status as an interested party with standing to protest and the timeliness of the protest;
    - A detailed description of the factual and legal basis (or bases) for protest, an explanation of any

---

[13] See Geodata Sys. Mgmt., Inc., B-416798, 2018 CPD ¶ 330 (Comp. Gen. Oct. 1, 2018) (dismissing pre-award protest filed 2 hours and 25 minutes after the deadline).

prejudice suffered by the protester, and copies of relevant documents supporting these assertions; and

- The ruling and relief requested from GAO.

If a protester believes that resolution of its protest is likely to involve confidential or proprietary information, it can also ask GAO to issue a protective order to shield this information from public disclosure. GAO might not enter a protective order for pre-award protests—because bids haven't been submitted, it's not always clear that confidential information will be involved. But if you think it will be, ask. Just keep in mind that, if a protective order is issued, only your counsel will receive the protected material—a protester itself likely will not be admitted to the protective order.

If there are documents that might be relevant to the protest grounds (say, for example, the agency's market research in a pre-award protest challenging the set-aside designation), the protest should also ask the agency to produce them.

- Where to file? In 2018, GAO implemented a new Electronic Protest Docketing System (or *EPDS*, for short), through which all protests must be filed. To do so, the protester (or its counsel) must register on EPDS and then upload the protest to the system. Before the protest is accepted, moreover, the protester will be directed to a different website to pay a filing fee.[14]

    Be aware! This registration and payment requirement can add a few extra minutes to the filing process. Don't wait until the last minute to try to file the protest—if it's late, it'll likely be dismissed.

Unlike an agency-level protest, a GAO protest isn't over after the initial protest is filed. Not by a long shot.

Thirty days after the protest is filed, the agency is obligated to provide its substantive response.[15] This response—called the "agency report"—is the factual and legal rebuttal to the protester's arguments. Importantly, the agency has to include a copy of "all

---

[14] At the time of publication, GAO's filing fee was $350.

[15] Oftentimes, the agency might elect to take a voluntary corrective action instead of responding. In a pre-award protest, this voluntary corrective action would probably involve revising the solicitation in some way.

relevant documents" with its report, including those asked for by the protester. 4 C.F.R. § 21.3(d).

But the agency doesn't get the last word. The protester must file comments on the agency report replying to the arguments therein within ten days. Importantly, filing comments isn't optional—GAO's rules make clear that the "protest shall be dismissed unless the protester files comments within the 10-day period, except where GAO has granted an extension or established a shorter period[.]" 4 C.F.R. § 21.3(i). These comments are essentially the protester's reply to the agency's rebuttal—with the agency's document production, the protester gets one last shot to argue why its protest should be sustained.[16]

After briefing is complete, GAO will take the matter under advisement and consider the parties' respective arguments. Its decision will come within 100-days from the date the protest is filed—which, when you think of it, is a remarkable feat

---

[16] Sometimes, the agency's document production will reveal grounds for a supplemental protest. In that case, the protest must be filed within 10 days from when it first learned (or should have learned) of the basis of protest. 4 C.F.R. § 21.2(a)(2). For each supplemental protest, GAO will establish a briefing schedule.

considering that each protest is nuanced and that GAO decides hundreds of protests every year.

With the procedures in mind, it's important to note the relatively high bar that a protest faces. GAO often notes that, because contracting officials are familiar with an agency's needs, the determination of how to meet those needs is generally up to the agency.[17] But importantly, this discretion isn't unlimited. If an offeror challenges a solicitation for being ambiguous, GAO will review the solicitation to determine whether the solicitation is detailed enough to allow offerors to compete intelligently and on a relatively equal basis.[18] And if the protest challenges an overly-restrictive solicitation, GAO will consider whether the solicitation achieves full and open competition; in general, a solicitation can include restrictive solicitation requirements only to the extent they are necessary to meet those needs.[19] Facing a protest arguing that a solicitation is unduly restrictive, the agency must

---

[17] See, e.g., Pitney Bowes, Inc., B-413876.2, 2017 CPD ¶ 56 (Comp. Gen. Feb. 13, 2017).

[18] See, e.g., AirTrak Travel et al., B-292101 et al., 2003 CPD ¶ 117 (Comp. Gen. June 30, 2003).

[19] See, e.g., Parcel 49C Ltd. P'ship, B-412552 et al., 2016 CPD ¶ 95 (Comp. Gen. Mar. 23, 2016).

demonstrate the specification is reasonably necessary to meet its needs.[20]

Without a doubt, pre-award GAO protests are a significant effort. But depending on the issue, they can absolutely be worthwhile: if successful, they might help shape the competition to make it more advantageous to your firm.

---

[20] See, e.g., Smith & Nephew, Inc., B-410453, 2015 CPD ¶ 90 (Comp. Gen. Jan. 2, 2015).

COURT OF FEDERAL CLAIMS

Now that we've discussed pre-award bid protests at GAO, let's briefly discuss pre-award protests at the Court of Federal Claims. When we first started outlining this *Handbook*, we didn't imagine discussing COFC pre-award protests much—they're not all that common. But as we sit here writing it, arguably the most high-profile bid protest currently pending is a pre-award protest at the Court of Federal Claims. In it, at least one would-be offeror challenges the Department of Defense's plan to issue the Joint Enterprise Defense Infrastructure (or *JEDI*) award to a single offeror, rather than naming multiple awardees. The stakes are enormous: the JEDI procurement seeks to make a $10 billion award for cloud computing infrastructure.[21]

Not every offeror will file a pre-award protest at the Court of Federal Claims. But if you have targeted a solicitation that's vital enough to your business, it might be worth the costs of doing so.

---

[21] See, e.g., Billy Mitchell, Oracle protests $10B JEDI cloud contract in Court of Federal Claims, Fedscoop.com, available at https://www.fedscoop.com/oracle-protests-10b-jedi-court-federal-claims/ (last accessed Dec. 20, 2018).

If you're considering it, there are a few points to contemplate. First, the timeliness rule: just like at GAO, a protest challenging the terms of the solicitation must be filed at the Court of Federal Claims before the deadline to submit proposals. If not, the objection will be considered waived.[22] Just as with GAO, the purpose of this deadline is to allow potential offerors to argue about the ground rules up to the point when the competition begins. After that, the rules are set—a protester can't sit on a pre-award challenge to the solicitation, then wait to challenge the impropriety until only after it loses out in the competition.

Second, the mechanics of a COFC protest: in many respects, a COFC challenge is akin to civil litigation against the government, just without prolonged discovery or a formal trial. As a protester, you'll have to file a complaint that details the factual and legal challenges to the solicitation. After it's received, the government will promptly produce the Administrative Record (or, basically, all the relevant documents) and, in rare instances, the Court might allow limited follow-up discovery. Once that production is complete, the parties will then brief the

---

[22] See, e.g., Blue & Gold Fleet, L.P. v. United States, 492 F.3d 1308, 1314–15 (Fed. Cir. 2007).

issues for the Court. This briefing is accomplished through the parties' respective motions for judgment on the administrative record, which is just a way of saying that the matter is essentially submitted for resolution based on the documentary evidence filed at the Court.

After briefing is completed, the Court will likely schedule oral argument. This argument, though, isn't a trial—the Court won't call any witnesses but, instead, the parties will argue their respective positions to the judge. Afterwards, the Court will issue a final written decision granting or denying the protest. This all takes place very quickly—usually over just a few months.

As you might imagine, a Court of Federal Claims protest can be an extensive endeavor. But filing a pre-award bid protest at the Court of Federal Claims might be worth it, particularly where an offeror believes it will be at a competitive disadvantage due to an objectionable solicitation requirement.

THE TAKEAWAY

Regardless of the forum, the key point to remember about a pre-award protest is when it must be filed: **challenges to the terms of a solicitation must be filed before the deadline to submit proposals.** Once that deadline passes, the ground rules for the solicitation are locked-in, and you can't subsequently argue they were unreasonable or unfair.

We see this rule trip up potential protesters all too frequently. Sometimes, we'll get a call from an offeror who lost an award because it interpreted the evaluation criteria differently than an agency. But a patently ambiguous solicitation provision—that is, an ambiguity that is obvious on the face of the solicitation—must be challenged as part of a pre-award protest.[23] So, too, must challenges to the solicitation's set-aside designation,[24] any requirement that unreasonably restricts

---

[23] See Pitney Bowes, Inc., B-416787, 2018 WL 6589433 (Comp. Gen. Dec. 6, 2018) ("An offeror that competes under a patently ambiguous solicitation does so at its own peril, and cannot later complain when the agency proceeds in a manner inconsistent with one of the possible interpretations.").

[24] See Spur Design, LLC, B-412245.3, 2016 CPD ¶ 62 (Comp. Gen. Feb. 24, 2016).

competition,[25] or any other potential solicitation flaws. The point is that if a solicitation is unclear or unfair in any respect, or if it includes any provision that might impede fair competition, consider raising this issue *before* you submit your bid—otherwise, it may be too late to object later.

If you'd like to bid on a solicitation that's either vague, restrictive, unfair, or otherwise improper, give thought to filing a pre-award protest. Sometimes, offerors don't want to file pre-award protest out of fear of upsetting the solicitation before submitting a bid. But that fear might be overstated: in our experience, contracting officers are professionals, and they understand that pre-award protests are simply part of the acquisition process.

More fundamentally, consider your odds of success if the solicitation impropriety *isn't* fixed. Too frequently, we've had prospective clients call to discuss an evaluation that resulted in an award to a competitor, arguing that the evaluation was unfair because of a vague or overly-restrictive solicitation requirement. Sometimes, it will be clear from the solicitation's questions and

---

[25] See Missouri Machinery & Engineering Co., B-403561, 2010 CPD ¶ 276 (Comp. Gen. Nov. 18, 2010).

answers that this impropriety was obvious on the face of the solicitation, as offerors asked the agency for clarity. Having received none, the offerors bid anyway and simply hoped for the best. When the interpretation goes against them, however, they might be left with an untimely challenge to the solicitation's terms.

In our (humble) opinion, it makes sense to try to address any solicitation improprieties before they negatively impact your chance at winning the award.

POST-AWARD BID PROTESTS

Having sorted out that the agency didn't want dark chocolate dog food, your company submitted a timely bid to provide *regular* dog food. But unfortunately, you were notified that your competitor received the award. After timely requesting a debriefing, you learned the agency found your proposal *unacceptable* for not presenting five past performance references, when the solicitation only called for three.

You might think that was unreasonable, and you would be right. The agency's improper evaluation of your proposal forms the basis for a viable post-award protest because it relied on unstated evaluation criteria in evaluating your proposal. Unlike a pre-award protest (which, again, challenges the terms of a solicitation), a post-award protest challenges the agency's evaluation of proposals.

> ### SIDEBAR
>
> The term "post-award protest" is a bit of a misnomer. Though the quintessential post-award protest comes—as the phrase implies—after the award, a post-award protest might actually be filed before the award is made. For example, if an offeror's proposal is eliminated early on in a phased evaluation (such as part of a competitive range cutoff determination), that offeror will need to challenge the evaluation as part of a post-award protest—even if the award has not yet been made.

After deciding to file a protest, the question then becomes which forum to file in.

GOVERNMENT ACCOUNTABILITY OFFICE

A post-award GAO protest is very similar, at least procedurally, to a pre-award protest:

- When to file? By now, the deadline to file a GAO protest should be familiar: if a debriefing is not required (or is not timely requested), a post-award GAO protest must be filed within 10 days from the date the basis of protest becomes known (or should have been known, if earlier). If a debriefing is required and timely requested, the protest is due within 10 days from the date the debriefing is received.[26] 4 C.F.R. § 21.2(a)(2).

    The importance of timely filing a bid protest cannot be overstated. *If a protest (pre-award or post-award) isn't timely filed, GAO will dismiss it—no matter how strong its arguments might be.* GAO has the right to hear an untimely protest when good cause is shown that it "raises issues

---

[26] A protest filed within 5 days of a properly-requested, required debriefing triggers the automatic stay of performance—meaning that, except in rare circumstances, the agency can't allow the new awardee to transition to performance until the protest is resolved.

significant to the procurement system," but GAO does not often avail itself of that opportunity.[27] Id. § 21.2(c).

- What to file? A post-award protest must contain the same information, in general, as a pre-award protest:
    - The protester's name, address, telephone and fax numbers, and email address;
    - Identification of the agency and the solicitation or contract number;
    - Information supporting the protester's status as an interested party with standing to protest and the timeliness of the protest;
    - A detailed explanation of the factual and legal basis (or bases) for protest, an explanation of any prejudice suffered by the protester, and copies of relevant documents supporting these assertions; and
    - The ruling and relief requested from GAO. In making this request, keep in mind that GAO isn't likely to recommend that the agency name the

---

[27] See DRS Tech. Servs., Inc., B-41573.2 et al., 2015 CPD ¶ 363 (Comp. Gen. Nov. 9, 2015).

protester the awardee; instead, GAO will likely recommend that the agency reevaluate proposals and, if necessary, make a new award determination.[28]

Additionally, a protester should consider asking GAO to issue a protective order as part of the protest. Doing so will not only shield the protester's confidential information from public disclosure, but it will also allow the protester's authorized representatives to access the agency's case file.[29] These documents will be tremendously important to the resolution of the protest—without accessing them, in fact, the protester will have great difficulty proving its case.

- Where to file? Like with a pre-award protest, post-award protests must be filed at GAO through EPDS. Again, be sure to start the filing process well in advance of GAO's 5:30 p.m. (Eastern) filing deadline. 4 C.F.R. § 21.0(f). If a

---

[28] The only instance that GAO might recommend an award to the protester is if there were only two offerors (the protester and the awardee), and the protest shows the awardee's proposal to have been unacceptable or otherwise unawardable.

[29] The protest should ask the agency to produce any specific documents that are relevant to the protest grounds.

protest is filed after 5:30 p.m., it will be considered filed on the following business day—which might make it one day too late.[30]

Beyond these initial filing mechanics, GAO's post-award protest resolution procedures will also proceed along the same track as a pre-award protest. Let's review:

The agency will produce its response to the protest (again, called the "agency report") within thirty days after the protest is filed. This response must include the agency's factual and legal arguments rebutting the protest, as well as copies of all relevant documents.

Within 10 days after receiving the agency report, the protester must file its comments. Failing to do so will result in the protest being dismissed. These comments are, essentially, the last word[31] in the protest: the protester has the opportunity to say why,

---

[30] See CWIS, LLC, B-416544, 2018 CPD ¶ 236 (Comp. Gen. July 12, 2018) (dismissing protest as untimely, when the protester encountered an error attempting to file in EPDS and, by the time the protest was filed, the 5:30 filing deadline had passed).

[31] Assuming, of course, that there isn't reason to file a supplemental protest. If there is, and if that supplemental protest is timely filed, there will also be additional briefing on that supplemental protest.

notwithstanding the agency's rebuttal, the protest should be sustained.

Once briefing has been completed, GAO will consider the arguments raised by the parties and issue its final decision within 100 days of the protest being filed.

EXAMPLE

On March 1, Innovative Technology received notice from the agency that its proposal—submitted under a negotiated acquisition, per FAR Part 15—was not named the awardee; instead, StatusQuo Technology was given the award. Innovative Technology requested its debriefing on March 2, and the agency provided this debriefing on March 10.

The debriefing revealed that the agency considered Innovative Technology's price to be unrealistically low. But because the solicitation did not warn offerors that prices would be evaluated for realism, Innovative Technology filed a post-award protest challenging the agency's price evaluation on March 15. Because this protest was filed within five days from the date of Innovative

Technology's required (and timely-requested) debriefing, it was timely and triggered an automatic stay of performance.

The agency timely files its report on April 14. As part of the agency's document production that accompanied the report, Innovative Technology learns of a new flaw in the evaluation: specifically, that the agency failed to consider StatusQuo's exception to a material solicitation requirement.

Innovative Technology must file its comments on the agency report before April 24. Additionally, Innovative Technology can file a supplemental protest challenging the evaluation of StatusQuo's proposal by this same date; if it chooses to do so, GAO will set deadlines to receive the agency's supplemental report and Innovative Technology's supplemental comments.

After this briefing is completed, GAO will take the matter under advisement. Its regulatory deadline to resolve the dispute—both the initial and supplemental protests—is June 23 (or 100 days after the protest was filed on March 15). And given the improper evaluation, there's a decent chance that GAO would sustain the

> protest and recommend the agency reevaluate proposals—this time sticking to the terms of the solicitation.

With these mechanics in mind, the fundamental question becomes: *are GAO protests effective?* The answer, oftentimes, is "yes."

Don't take our word for it. Every year, GAO publishes its bid protest statistics, and the results are quite telling and fairly consistent: of the approximate 2500 protests filed annually, GAO decides around 600 on the merits (the remainder are resolved prior to a final decision—either from being dismissed due to a flaw in the protest itself, or following resolution via agency corrective action or through alternative dispute resolution). Of these, GAO historically sustains around 15% of protests.[32]

This number is, in itself, fairly impressive: nearly 1 in 6 filed protests is sustained on the merits. But GAO considers around *half* of the protests filed to be effective—that is, about 45% of the protests filed at GAO annually result in some type of

---

[32] Over the past few years, the sustain rate has fluctuated between 12% and 23%.

favorable result to the protester, either through voluntary corrective action by the agency or a sustained decision on the merits, a promising figure if you find yourself in the position of a protester.[33]

Which arguments are most likely to be successful? Each bid protest is different, but GAO's annual bid protest report offers guidance. According to GAO, the arguments that are most frequently successful cogently argue that the evaluation was unreasonable in some respect.

- <u>Unreasonable technical evaluation.</u> One of the most successful arguments is when a protester can argue that the agency's technical evaluation was flawed in some way—either its proposal was improperly downgraded in a manner that prejudiced its chance at receiving the award, or the awardee's proposal was credited in a manner that it shouldn't have been. For example, in <u>CR/ZWS LLS</u>, B-414766 <u>et al.</u>, 2017 CPD ¶ 288 (Comp. Gen. Sept. 13, 2017), the agency improperly awarded a contract to a company, despite the fact that the company's management plan did

---

[33] Unfortunately, GAO doesn't track whether protests are "effective" in the sense of whether the protester actually ended up receiving the award.

not address all the items required by the solicitation. GAO sustained the protest, finding that the awardee's failure to address all the solicitation requirements meant that its proposal should have been found unacceptable.

- <u>Unreasonable cost evaluation.</u> Price and cost evaluations can be fertile ground for protest. The reason is simple: math is hard. Beyond that, preparing prices (or costs, in a cost-reimbursable contract) can be *very* complicated—so evaluating them can be difficult, too. If the agency gets a simple calculation wrong, or if it doesn't have all the information needed, the whole evaluation can be off. That's what happened in <u>Marine Hydraulics International, Inc.</u>, B-403386 <u>et al.</u>, 2010 CPD ¶ 255 (Comp. Gen. Nov. 3, 2010), when GAO sustained a protest challenging a cost realism evaluation because the agency improperly adjusted the protester's cost upward in a manner that wasn't supported by the protester's proposed effort.

- <u>Flawed past performance evaluation.</u> The purpose of a past performance evaluation is to assess the confidence that an offeror will successfully perform the solicited effort based on its recent history of performing similar efforts. If the agency's evaluation doesn't follow the requirements, GAO will sustain a protest challenging the past performance evaluation. In MLU Services, Inc., B-414555.3 et al., 2017 CPD ¶ 225 (Comp. Gen. July 17, 2017), for example, the agency credited the awardee with the past performance of an affiliated company. Because this affiliate would not actually perform any work under the contract, however, the agency should not have credited the awardee with its performance. Thus, GAO sustained the protest based on this flawed evaluation.

- Misleading discussions. If an agency opens discussions with one offeror, or otherwise allows that offeror the opportunity to fix issues with its proposal, it generally must allow every other offeror in the competitive range that same opportunity. If it doesn't, GAO will sustain a protest. See Paragon Tech. Grp., Inc., B-412636 et al., 2016 CPD ¶ 113 (Comp. Gen. Apr. 22, 2016) (sustaining protest where the agency's discussion questions did not address the agency's true concern with the offeror's proposal).

- <u>Flawed selection decision.</u> Sometimes, an agency departs from the stated evaluation scheme (like by effectively converting a best value solicitation into a lowest-price technically-acceptable award) or doesn't consider the merits of one proposal compared to another. <u>VariQ Corporation</u>, B-414650.11 <u>et al.</u>, 2018 CPD ¶ 199 (Comp. Gen. May 30, 2018) is an example. In that case, the agency didn't weigh the protester's strengths as heavily as it did the awardee's, even though the strengths were for similar aspects of the offerors' proposals. Because this disparate consideration resulted in a lower rating for the protester, GAO sustained the protest.

SIDEBAR

Protests aren't limited to raising only one argument. Often, protests will raise several different arguments attacking the evaluation. Some of these arguments may be stronger than others, but given GAO's strict timeliness rules, offerors should be prepared to raise every supportable argument in its protest.

Now that we've addressed the arguments most likely to succeed at GAO, let's discuss those almost certainly doomed to fail:

- <u>Complaints about the debriefing.</u> If an agency fails to provide the information required as part of a debriefing, the disappointed offeror might want to protest at GAO. But a deficient debriefing is not, in itself, a valid basis of protest.

- <u>Small business issues.</u> Issues relating to an awardee's size or socio-economic eligibility must be protested to the SBA, not GAO. Be aware: these protests have even tighter deadlines than GAO protests, so be sure to act fast.

- <u>Bias.</u> Sometimes, it seems like a contracting officer set out to give the award to your competitor and had no interest in giving you a fair shot. Though there could be reason to protest, allegations of bias probably shouldn't be raised. "Government officials are presumed to act in good faith," so a protester alleging bias must present "convincing proof" in support of its arguments—inference or supposition simply won't cut it. <u>Sevatec, Inc.</u>, B-416617 et al., 2018 CPD ¶ 379 (Comp. Gen. Nov. 1, 2018). Unless you have this convincing proof—something like an email from the contracting officer saying "I am biased against you, and that's why you lost this award"—raising a claim of bias might serve only to undercut your other (hopefully better) arguments.

That's it: the basics about post-award GAO bid protests. Next, we'll discuss post-award protests at the Court of Federal Claims.

COURT OF FEDERAL CLAIMS

If a GAO protest isn't successful, you might consider filing another protest at the Court of Federal Claims.[34] But contrary to a persistent belief, a COFC bid protest isn't an *appeal* of a GAO bid protest decision. Instead, the Court will *separately* evaluate whether the agency's evaluation and award decisions were arbitrary or capricious, or otherwise violated any applicable procurement statute or regulation; if so, and if the error was prejudicial, the Court will sustain the protest. It will make this determination independent of GAO's position on the matter.

COFC protests can, as noted above, be quite intensive. Post-award protests proceed much in the same way as a pre-award protest. But given the fact that a post-award protest challenges the evaluation and award, the Administrative Record will probably be more robust than it would be in a pre-award protest. This means that the briefing might be more extensive, and

---

[34] As we discussed earlier, a protest can initially be filed at the Court of Federal Claims, too. But just keep in mind that, once a protest is filed at the Court of Federal Claims, a protester can't then protest at GAO.

the protester might have more information to support its arguments that the evaluation was flawed.

To be successful in a post-award COFC protest, a protester must show that the agency's evaluation was arbitrary and capricious, or that it otherwise violated an applicable procurement statute or regulation. This standard of review—conducted under the Administrative Procedure Act[35]—is "exceedingly narrow."[36] The Court will deny a protest if the agency articulates a "rational connection between the facts found and the choice made."[37] Even if a protester shows a flaw in the evaluation, it must then show that the agency's error was prejudicial—that is, the protester must show that, absent the error, it would have stood a substantial chance at receiving the award.[38]

Given this high standard, one can imagine that COFC protests tend not to be as effective as GAO protests. The data

---

[35]   5 U.S.C. § 706.

[36]   Crewzers Fire Crew Transport, Inc. v. United States, 98 Fed. Cl. 71, 76 (2011).

[37]   Motor Vehicle Mfrs. Ass'n v. State Farm Mut. Auto. Ins. Co., 463 U.S. 29, 43 (1983).

[38]   JWK Int'l Corp. v. United States, 279 F.3d 985, 988 (Fed. Cir. 2002).

shows this to be true . . . sort of. According to a recent study, COFC protests aren't nearly as common as GAO protests.

Responding to an instruction from Congress, the Department of Defense commissioned a comprehensive study on the effect of bid protests on the acquisition process.[39] The results of this study were published in early 2018, and the findings are pretty interesting. For example, while a couple thousand GAO bid protests are filed annually, COFC protests are much less frequent: from 2008 until mid-2017, only about 950 bid protests *in total* were filed at the Court. These protests involve a slew of acquisitions—ranging from multi-million dollar procurements, to relatively small contracts valued at less than $100,000. The report suggests, however, that COFC protests are a little less effective than GAO protests, as only about 9% of the analyzed COFC protests were sustained (compared to GAO's annual sustain rate of approximately 15%).[40]

---

[39] E.g., Steven Koprince, "DoD Bid Protests Are 'Exceedingly Uncommon,' New Study Finds," SmallGovCon.com (published Jan. 5, 2018; last accessed Dec. 31, 2018).

[40] Rand Corporation's report—entitled "Assessing Bid Protests of U.S. Department of Defense Procurements"—can be found at https://www.rand.org/pubs/research_reports/RR2356.html. It's a very thorough read on the impact of bid protests.

The Court of Federal Claims' lower sustain rate, however, does not necessarily mean that these protests aren't worth considering. Keep in mind that this metric doesn't necessarily track a protest's effectiveness—like at GAO, COFC protests are sometimes voluntarily dismissed due to corrective action, so the overall effectiveness rate is likely higher than the sustain rate. Also, keep in mind the usual progression of a bid protest: protesters will oftentimes first file at GAO, then proceed to the Court of Federal claims only if that protest isn't successful. This progression naturally means that the most obviously successful protests will, in many cases, have already been weeded out before a protest is filed at the Court of Federal Claims. But even still, a healthy chunk of COFC protests end up being sustained on their merits.

Like with GAO protests, the likelihood of success in a COFC protest entirely depends on the specific protest arguments raised and the content of the agency's underlying documentation. Depending on your circumstance, filing a COFC protest (or a GAO protest, or both) could end up giving your company another chance at winning a contract.

INTERVENTION: DEFENDING YOUR AWARD

Up to now, this *Handbook* has discussed bid protests from the standpoint of a disappointed offeror seeking to challenge an evaluation or award. But there's a reverse side to the bid protest coin: that of a successful awardee seeking to defend its award.

In the event your award is protested at GAO or the Court of Federal Claims, you'll likely have the right to intervene, which allows you to be a party to the protest and argue that, contrary to the protester's protestations, the evaluation and award were proper. Though it is not required, awardees should give serious consideration to intervening. While the agency will be the primary voice defending its decision, sometimes an intervenor is able to successfully argue that a protest should be dismissed or present supplemental arguments in support of an agency's briefing that ultimately help preserve its award.

You might ask: *Why should I spend the time and money intervening when the agency will just defend my award?* There are a lot of reasons, really. For starters, it's your right to do so, and the agency isn't obligated to protect your award. Instead, the agency might think that getting rid of the protest as quickly as possible is most important and take a corrective action that it otherwise might not need to if the protest was dismissed or denied. Beyond that, agency personnel are often overworked, so they might not be able to devote the time needed to analyze and defend an award (particularly if an award is complex). Intervening in a protest will give you, as the awardee, the right to supplement the agency's positions or raise any others it might've overlooked. Another reason is that intervening might help the agency view your company early on as a partner it can rely upon—as your company is about to embark on contract performance that might last several years, this wouldn't be a bad first impression to make.

The process of intervening is relatively straightforward: you'll simply need to file a request to intervene at GAO, or a more formal motion to intervene at the Court of Federal Claims. But so long as your company is the awardee under the solicitation being protested, this request shouldn't be controversial. Once granted, you'll have access to the agency's document production (through your counsel, admitted to the protective order,) and will be able to submit briefing to GAO or the Court. In other words, your company will have a seat at the table as the issues in the protest are being resolved.

***

So that's the skinny about bid protests. Remember, every solicitation is unique, so the grounds for protest—and the chances of success—will change with each circumstance. Below, though, we wanted to offer a few tips to hopefully increase the odds of success:

1. *Get counsel . . . as soon as possible.* Sure, we're biased. But we believe that competent counsel can help the bid protest process go much smoother. Experienced counsel help make the best arguments possible; in fact, RAND Corporation's bid protest report says that protests filed through counsel have higher effectiveness and sustained rates than those filed *pro se*. This makes sense, as outside counsel can be admitted to a protective order, through which they will have access to the agency's protected documents. These documents might include support for the initial protest arguments or even reveal supplemental arguments. And, if you're filing at the Court of Federal Claims, you'll have to have counsel, as the Court requires protesters to appear through admitted counsel.

If at all possible, we think it's a good idea for protesters (or intervenors, for that matter) to be represented by counsel.

Regardless of whether you obtain counsel, however, remember to act fast. GAO's bid protest deadlines are very short. The longer you wait, the less time you'll have to develop the strongest arguments possible.

2. *Make the most of your debriefing.* Effective protests often start with the debriefing. We discussed how to make the most of your debriefing in the previous Part, but it's worth repeating here. Before the debriefing, refamiliarize yourself with the solicitation and offer. Discuss the solicitation with your proposal team. Develop cogent, insightful questions that get to the heart of your proposal and the evaluation.

3. *Understand your arguments.* After the debriefing, consider whether the agency properly evaluated your effort. If not, you might have a basis to protest.

Keep in mind, though, that not every evaluation error will lead to a successful protest. That is, GAO and the Court of Federal Claims both give deference to an agency's reasonable procurement-related decisions. In essence, a tie goes to the agency. In our practice, we'll sometimes counsel prospective clients to not file a protest—because the arguments would not likely be sustained by GAO or the Court, we'd counsel against spending the time (and money) on a bid protest. This is an important lesson for any bid protest guide: sometimes, the best thing to do is to take your lumps and devote your energy to the next bid.

4. *Maintain a professional tone.* Filing a protest is a big decision. Sometimes, would-be protesters are concerned that the protest might destroy their relationship with the agency. Our thought, though, is that a protest doesn't have to: most contracting officials understand that protests are part of the acquisition process. That said, a protest is an adversarial action. To minimize any hard feelings, a protester should maintain a professional and civil tone throughout the protest process . . . as hard as that might sometimes be.

5. *Manage your expectations.* Along these same lines, a protester should keep its expectations in check. A successful protest probably won't guarantee that the protester receives the award; rather, it will give the protest a second chance at the award, usually through a reevaluation. If a protester goes into a protest expecting to receive the award, it is likely to end up disappointed—even if its protest is successful.

6. *Implement lessons learned.* The value of a protest goes far beyond the particular acquisition at issue. Sometimes, GAO will say that a protester's proposal didn't clearly articulate its approach or was not otherwise deserving of particular strengths. Take this information to heart: just like with its debriefing, a protester should develop an after-protest action plan, to help implement the lessons learned into future proposals.

CONCLUSION

As this *Handbook* hopefully suggests, the decision whether to file a bid protest is not one to take lightly. No two bid protests are alike, and the likelihood of success for any protest depends on the specific, unique facts under that procurement. We suggest making the most of your debriefing *and* discussing the issues with counsel as early as you can. But at the end of the day, we hope that decision is made somewhat easier by our discussion in this *Handbook*.

ACRONYMS ARE FUN: ACRONYM LIST

Federal government contracting is full of acronyms—and so is this *Handbook*. Please find below definitions for some of the acronyms you may encounter reading this *Handbook*.

C.F.R. Code of Federal Regulations. This is where specific government regulations are codified. For example, Title 4 of the Code of Federal Regulations includes regulations relating to the Government Accountability Office. Beginning at Chapter 21, Title 4 sets out GAO's bid protest regulations.

COFC. Court of Federal Claims. This is a federal court that has jurisdiction to consider bid protests and other actions relating to federal procurements.

DoD. Department of Defense. The Department of Defense makes up about half of federal spending each year, making it the largest federal purchaser of goods and services.

EPDS. Electronic Protest Docketing System. EPDS is GAO's new electronic protest filing system; as of 2018, all bid protests must be filed through EPDS.

FAA. Federal Aviation Administration. The Federal Aviation Administration is exempted from the Competition in Contracting Act, so it's not subject to GAO's bid protest jurisdiction. Instead, the FAA has its own protest resolution processes, which are governed by the FAA's Office of Dispute Resolution for Acquisition.

FAR. Federal Acquisition Regulations. The FAR sets forth detailed regulations governing most federal procurements. Agencies often have their own FAR supplements, which further apply to their specific procurements.

GAO. Government Accountability Office. GAO has jurisdiction to consider most type of bid protests and, on average, considers about 2500 actions each year. Because GAO is an arm of Congress, it cannot actually direct an agency to take any specific action in response to a protest; instead, GAO makes recommendations to agencies and, the vast majority of the time, agencies follow them.

GSA. General Services Administration. Among GSA's functions is its administration of Schedule contracts, through which the government purchase many goods and services. These Schedule contracts have particular bid protest rules and requirements.

NAICS. North American Industry Classification System. NAICS codes are developed by the Census Bureau for each industry area and are assigned by the contracting officer to each solicitation (based on the solicitation's primary requirements). The Small Business Administration develops size standards that correspond to each NAICS code. To qualify as a small business under a particular solicitation, an entity's size must fall under the size standard for the NAICS code assigned to the solicitation.

NDAA. National Defense Authorization Act. Through the NDAA, Congress sets the annual spending priorities for the Department of Defense. Oftentimes, the Act includes specific acquisition-related provisions, which impact federal procurements going forward.

OHA. Office of Hearings and Appeals. Part of the SBA, the OHA considers appeals of size protests and socio-economic protest matters.

PWS. Performance Work Statement. The PWS (or statement of work) includes the technical objectives of the solicitation and the work sought by the agency.

SBA. Small Business Administration. The SBA is charged with advancing the interests of small businesses in the federal government. As part of this role, the SBA sets goals for small business participation in prime contracting, and has developed regulations governing the requirements for small business contracting.

SDVOSB. Service-Disabled Veteran-Owned Small Business. An SDVOSB is a small business that is at least 51% owned and controlled by a service-disabled veteran. As of this writing, the SBA has established a 3% SDVOSB prime contracting goal for the federal government.

ABOUT THE AUTHORS

Matthew T. Schoonover

is a partner at Koprince Law LLC, where he counsels clients on the unique issues they face as federal government contractors. In addition to advising clients about regulatory and compliance issues (including under the FAR and SBA's, DOD's, and the VA's regulations), Matt represents contractors in bid protests (at GAO and the Court of Federal Claims), size and socio-economic category protests and appeals, and in claims and appeals matters under the Contract Disputes Act.

Matt has been honored to present on government contracting legal issues to a variety of audiences, including at several small business and veterans' contracting seminars. He has also been quoted in articles appearing in Bloomberg.com, Law360.com, Westlaw Journal, and Contract Management magazine. You can also read Matt's government contracting posts on SmallGovCon.com, including his 5 Things You Should Know series.

No matter the issue, Matt enjoys learning about prospective clients' industries and businesses. You can follow Matt on Twitter *@mtschoonover* or email him at *mschoonover@koprince.com*.

Matthew P. Moriarty

is a Senior Associate at Koprince Law LLC, where he exclusively practices federal government contracting law. Matt works with clients on litigation matters in various forums, including the Government Accountability Office, U.S. Small Business Administration, and the U.S. Court of Federal Claims, among others. He also assists clients with transactional issues, from numerous business-to-business relationships to compliance with various socioeconomic statutes and regulations. Matt is well-versed in the entire federal contracting regulatory landscape.

Matt has been a speaker at several federal government contracting events and has been quoted in Law360.com, the Washington Business Journal, and The Capitol Forum. Matt is also a frequent contributor to the government contracting blog SmallGovCon.com.

Matt enjoys working with small businesses to help them solve their problems. You can follow Matt on Twitter *@MoriartyGovCon* or email him at *mmoriarty@koprince.com*.

LEGAL SOLUTIONS FOR GOVERNMENT CONTRACTORS

Koprince Law LLC

When government contracting is the lifeblood of your business, you owe it to yourself to work with attorneys who understand the government's complex rules, regulations, and processes for its contractors.

Koprince Law LLC provides comprehensive legal solutions to government contractors. Period. We don't pretend to be everything to everyone. Instead, we focus on being very good at one thing—government contracts law.

Contact us:

(785) 200-8919   www.koprince.com   info@koprince.com

SMALLGOVCON

SmallGovCon is a blog providing legal news, notes, and commentary of interest to small government contractors. Written in plain English by the government contracts attorneys of Koprince Law LLC, *SmallGovCon* covers regulatory updates, bid protests, size appeals, federal court decisions, and much more. Visit *smallgovcon.com* to check out our posts and sign up for our free monthly electronic newsletter.

Made in the USA
Middletown, DE
30 December 2019